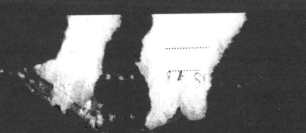

# How to go
# FISHING
## and Catch Fish!

## Gareth Purnell

W
FRANKLIN WATTS
LONDON•SYDNEY

First published in 2007
by Franklin Watts

Copyright © Franklin Watts 2007
Franklin Watts
338 Euston Road
London NW1 3BH

Franklin Watts Australia
Level 17/207 Kent Street
Sydney, NSW 2000

Series editor: Jeremy Smith
Designer: Jason Billin
Photography: Gareth Purnell unless indicated

Acknowledgements: Iconotec/Alamy: P5cl. Corbis/Phil Schermeister P27br, P28b.
Ken Kaminesky/Take2 Productions/Corbis: P28t.

A CIP catalogue record for this book
is available from the British Library.

Dewey no (where applicable) 799. 1'1
ISBN: 978 0 7496 7352 9

Printed in China.

Franklin Watts is a division of Hachette Children's Books.

# Contents

# Introduction

Fishing (also called angling) is one of the oldest sports in the world. It is a great way to spend the day, and is popular with millions of people of all ages. It gives you a chance to spend time outdoors, and to get involved with nature. Some anglers return the fish they catch to the water while others take their catch home for dinner.

*A young boy proudly displays a carp he has caught for the cameras.*

## Types of fishing

There are many different types of fishing. Sea anglers catch fish from saltwater. Game anglers fish for freshwater species like trout and salmon. Coarse anglers fish for any other type of freshwater fish.

Coarse fishing is the most popular type of fishing with amateur anglers and this book concentrates on this form of angling.

## Getting started

You might have always wanted to go fishing, but simply don't know where to start. There are lots of different ways to go fishing, and they don't have to be complicated. Anyone can go fishing using a few simple techniques and basic equipment.

This book introduces you to three of the most popular ways to catch fish - float fishing, leger fishing and pole fishing. It will also tell you how to catch fish safely, and how to return them to the water unharmed if you do not wish to take them home to eat.

*This father and son are preparing to go sea angling from the side of this pier.*

# What to catch?

## Chub

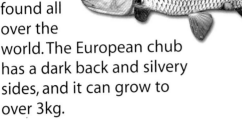

Chub are found all over the world. The European chub has a dark back and silvery sides, and it can grow to over 3kg.

## Roach

Big roach (fish over 450g) are considered to be the hardest of all species to catch. Roach have silvery scales and in clear water conditions their fins are tipped with red.

## Pike

A ferocious predator, the pike can grow to over 15kg. Long and lean, it is built for sudden bursts of speed, which it uses to dart out of cover to ambush prey.

## Bass

This silvery fish is popular in Europe and the United States. The large-mouthed bass prefers muddy, weedy water and grows to 7.5kg. The small-mouthed bass likes clear, rocky lakes and grows to about 3kg.

## Carp

This fish can be a number of colours and is popular with anglers in Europe. The largest carp caught weighed over 30kg. In Australia and the USA, many people consider the carp to be a pest.

## Wels catfish

This freshwater fish has a long, scaleless body a bit like an eel, and can grow to over 75kg. It is a predator and a scavenger but rests during the day. Its poor eyesight means it relies on its long feelers to seek out food.

## Perch

The perch is found all over Europe and across much of the US and Canada. It can grow to almost 2kg, and is easy to recognise with its spiky fin and vertical stripes.

## DID YOU KNOW?

The International Game Fish Association All Tackle record for the Wels catfish is a monster of 85kg. It was caught in Italy's River Mincio in 2006.

## Other species to catch

**Bream** - European fish with deep bronze sides

**Rudd** - Fish with golden flanks and flame-red fins

**Tench** - European fish with red eyes, green or brown flanks and tiny scales

**Zander** - European predator with greenish back and white belly. Hunts in low light

**Barbel** - European fish with brown colouring and reddish fins. Powerful fish that lives in rivers and fast-moving waters

# Where to fish

If you want to start fishing, the first thing to decide is where to fish. Different species live in different places. Ask your local tackle shop (a place that sells fishing equipment) where the best spots are. You will need a ticket or permit to fish in some places and you cannot fish during closed seasons (a time of the year when fish lay their eggs).

## Canals

A canal is an artificial waterway used by boats called barges. Many fish like to live in canals, too, so they are good places to go angling. Small fish like roach, skimmers and gudgeon, as well as carp, pike and zander, can all be found here. On summer days, however, boat traffic coming and going through canals can cause problems for anglers.

## Still waters

Natural still waters (waters without a visible current such as lakes and reservoirs) are full of fish. In Europe, this often means still waters hold plenty of bream, roach, perch, pike and some carp. In Canada and the US, natural still waters hold a variety of panfish, along with bass, pike and trout. Some privately owned still waters are stocked and can be filled with a variety of freshwater fish species.

## Rivers

Rivers are wonderful places to fish, and you can catch chub, perch, roach, minnows, grayling and dace, barbel carp and tench. Angling clubs may control certain stretches of rivers, but you usually don't have to buy a ticket in advance.

## TOP TIP

Fish like to visit places where they feel safe again and again. If you can find fish in a certain area on one day, it is likely they will be there the next. Look for places where trees overhang the water, where there are weeds or lily beds, or features such as bridges.

# Rods and reels

Once you have found a place to fish, the next step is to get kitted up. There is such a huge selection of rods, reels and accessories available that it is easy to get confused. Many ready-made starter kits have lines, rods and hooks that will be no use to you at all. The best idea is to go to your nearest tackle shop with an experienced angler, or talk to a tackle dealer about what sort of fishing you would like to do.

## Rods

There are rods for every type of angling. Most are made of carbon, and their name will give you a clue as to what they are used for. For example, a pike rod is meant for catching pike.

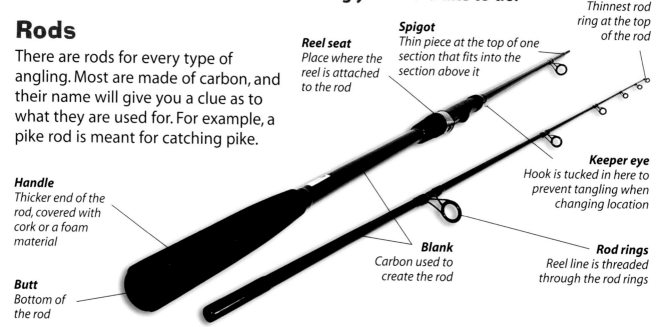

**Reel seat**
Place where the reel is attached to the rod

**Spigot**
Thin piece at the top of one section that fits into the section above it

**Tip eye**
Thinnest rod ring at the top of the rod

**Keeper eye**
Hook is tucked in here to prevent tangling when changing location

**Rod rings**
Reel line is threaded through the rod rings

**Blank**
Carbon used to create the rod

**Handle**
Thicker end of the rod, covered with cork or a foam material

**Butt**
Bottom of the rod

## Putting a rod together

Rods come in two or three pieces which have solid ends which thread into the wider hollow ends of the sections above.

**1 To put a rod together**, line up the the solid ends with the hollow ends, and push into the hollow end until the parts lock.

**2 As you push** the joints together, make sure the rings on the rod all line up like this.

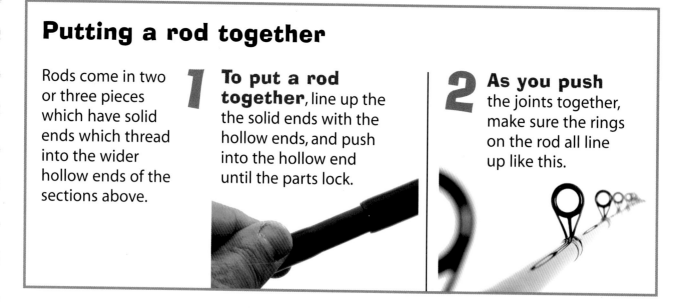

# Reels

Four main types of reel are used in coarse fishing, but the fixed spool is best for beginners.

**Spool**
Area where line is wound around

**Roller**
Line runs through roller when you turn the handle

**Foot**
Attachment that connects the reel to the rod

**Handle**
Used to wind line onto the spool

**Button**
Pressed to remove the spool and change to another

**Anti-Reverse Button**
Flicked to stop the handle from going backwards

**Drag/clutch**
Device that is turned to let line out when you have a fish on the end of your hook, to prevent the line from breaking

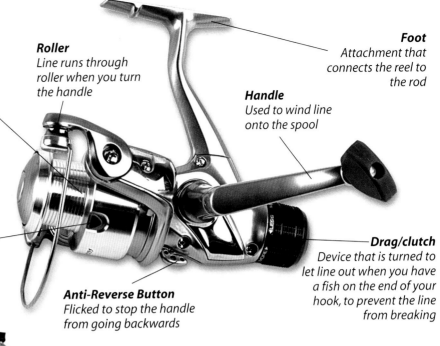

*The reel clips onto the rod at the reel seat.*

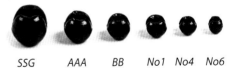

# Lines

Fishing line comes in different strengths. Anglers usually use 1.5kg line for float fishing and 3.2kg line for leger fishing. Never use worn line as it will be easier for a fish to snap it and escape.

# Split Shot

Weights, called split shots, are used to hold down floats (see page 18) in the water. Pinching a spilt shot on to a line using your fingers holds it in place. The shots shown below are the standard sizes for coarse fishing.

SSG   AAA   BB   No1   No4   No6

# Hooks

There are two kinds of hooks – 'eyed' hooks and 'spade-end' hooks. Both come in either barbed or barbless forms. Eyed hooks are tied onto the line with the knot sitting above the eye. With spade-end hooks, the knot is below the spade-shaped, flattened end.

*eyed barbless hook*

*eyed barbed hook*

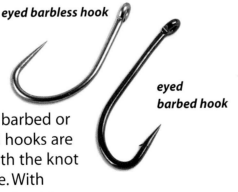

*The line, float and hook are referred to as the rig, and are fitted together as shown here.*

main line
rubber stopper
slip float
split shots
swivel
wire leader
hook

# How to load a reel

To put a line onto a reel correctly you must load the line right to the edge of the spool. This will ensure that whenever you cast your line it will be smooth and accurate. For deep spools you will need more than 100m (330ft) of line.

**1** **Attach** your reel to the handle of your rod by placing the foot into the fittings.

**2** **Pass** the loose end of the spool of line through the first ring on the rod down towards the reel.

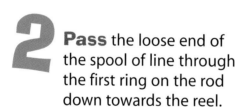

**3** **Open** the bale arm of your reel so that it points to the rod tip. Push the button at the top of the spool on your reel to release it. Put the rod down and tie the line onto the spool using any knot.

## KIT BITS

Your reel will have a lever underneath the body. This is used to engage and disengage the anti-reverse, to allow or stop the reel from turning backwards.

**4** **Trim** the knot so there is no long tag end. Then position the knot at the bottom of the spool as shown. Wind the line on by a few turns by hand to cover the knot.

**5** **Drop** the spool of line you wish to load into a bowl of water. The water will stop the spool from overrunning and tangling as you wind it on. Replace the spool onto your reel until it clicks into place and close the bale arm so that it's back in the original position.

**6** **Load** the line so that it sits right to the edge of the spool as illustrated. Cut the line when you reach this point. You're now ready to thread the line through the rings.

## DID YOU KNOW?

There are examples of Oriental paintings that depict Chinese fishermen using reels of various sizes that date to the twelfth century.

# Essential knots

Catching a fish takes a lot of effort and it would be a disaster to let one get away because your knot comes untied. These simple sequence of knots will ensure this does not happen to you.

These are the knots used to attach a hook to a length of line (the hook length) and the hooklength to the main line.

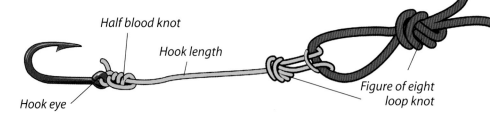

Half blood knot

Hook length

Hook eye

Figure of eight loop knot

---

## Part 1: The half blood knot

Half blood knots are simple, reliable knots. They can be used to make a hooklength - a short piece of line that has a fishing hook on the end of it.

**1** Thread the line through the eye and double up above it.

**2** Twist the hook around eight times.

**3** Keep the twists tight and grab the loose end.

**4** Push it through the lowest loop between the top of the eye and the first twist.

**5** Push the loose end through the loop you have made. This is the 'tuck'.

**6** Dampen the knot with spit and start to tighten the knot down above the eye.

**7** With the knot formed, pull it down to the eye.

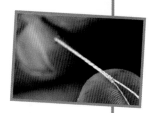

**8** Hold the knot tight for three seconds, then trim off.

# Part 2: The figure of eight loop

Once you have made your hooklength, you need to make a loop in the end of both this line and your main fishing line. These will be knotted together in Part 3 (see below).

**1** Form a simple loop in the end of the mainline.

**5** Now tuck the small loop into the larger loop.

**2** Hook the loop over itself.

**6** If done correctly the figure of eight will form as you tighten up.

**3** Put your index finger into the large loop and twist it around twice.

**7** Add some spit to the figure of eight and tighten up.

**4** Make another half twist – this is important.

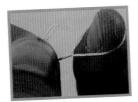

**8** Trim the knot tight and you have the strongest hooklength loop in the business.

# Part 3: The loop to loop knot

To finish off, you need to attach your hooklength to your main line using a loop to loop knot.

**1** Place your hooklength loop over the mainline loop.

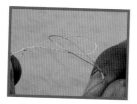

**3** When you pull tight the loop should entwine.

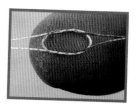

**2** Now thread the hook through the mainline loop the other way.

## DID YOU KNOW?

The ancient Greeks used fishing knots to catch fish over two thousand years ago.

# Bait guide

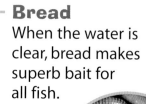

Fish are usually caught by lowering a piece of bait on the end of a line in to the water. The baits listed here are all great for catching non-predatory fish. To catch predatory fish you need small fish called livebait (see pages 22-23).

### Maggots
These are the grubs of the bluebottle flies. All species of fish, large and small will go for maggots as bait.

### Bread
When the water is clear, bread makes superb bait for all fish.

### Pinkies
These are grubs of the greenbottle fly, and are about half the size of maggots. They make excellent bait for smaller fish.

### Worms
A lobworm is great for catching big fish from rivers after there has been a flood and the water is not clear. Dendrabaena are cheaper and can be used to catch tench, bream, carp and perch.

### Squatts
The grubs of the housefly, these are about one-third the size of a pinkie. They are very useful bait for catching small fish in winter.

### Boilies
You can buy ready-made boilies in many different flavours or you can buy powdered mixes to make your own. Boilies make great bait for big fish.

### Casters
These are the chrysalis stage before the maggot becomes a fly. Casters make superb bait. If you store them in water they will sink, but if you keep them in the open air they will float.

### Pellets
Darker pellets are better in coloured water, lighter pellets in clear water. Expander pellets are pellets that need to be soaked before fishing then pumped in a pellet pump to make them sink under the water.

## Luncheon Meat

Luncheon meat cut into cubes makes good bait.

## Sweetcorn

This tasty bait will attract virtually every kind of fish.

## Hemp

Hemp seeds must be boiled first until they sink and the shells turn dark. They are usually used to attract fish that feed on the bottom of the water.

FRENZIED HEMPSEED

## Groundbait

This bait is used to tempt fish to your fishing area. Groundbait is made of ingredients such as bread and biscuits.

# How to hook a maggot

**1** Select a maggot with a clear black feeding sack in its head (the pointed end).

**2** Hold the maggot by the pointed end in one hand and your hook in the other.

**3** Push the point of the hook just into the blunt end where there are two black dots.

**4** The hooked maggot should wriggle. If it is damaged at all, try again with another maggot.

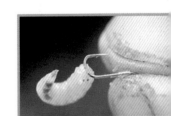

# HOOK AND BAIT GUIDE

| Hook size | Bait |
| --- | --- |
| 24 | Squatts |
| 22 | Pinkies |
| 20 | Maggots, breadpunch |
| 18 | Caster, double maggot, hemp seed |
| 16 | Double caster, pieces of worm, single corn, soft pellet |
| 14 | Double corn, whole worm |
| 12 | Breadflake, pieces of lobworm |
| 10 | Breadflake, luncheon meat, paste, small boilie |
| 8 | Boilie, hair rigged pellet |
| 6 | Whole lobworm, large boilie |

# How to cast

To increase your chances of catching a fish you need to be able to cast your line away from the bank. It is best to cast your line straight over your head. Never cast with the rod to your side (shown right).

**1** Wind the handle towards you to let the line off the reel until your rig hangs about 60–90cm (2–3ft) down from the tip of the rod. This girl has a swimfeeder attached to her line (see pages 20-21).

**2** Open the bale arm on the reel and trap the line with your finger, so no more lines runs off.

**3** Keep the bale arm open and the line trapped with your finger. Look around to make sure no one is standing right behind you and swing the rod back directly over your head.

**4** Place your hand on the very bottom of the handle.

## KIT BITS

The spool on your reel should have a line clip. This is used to ensure you are always casting the same distance.

**5** Point the bottom end of the rod where you want the rig to go, lining it up with your eyes.

**6** Punch the rod forward by pushing it away from you with your top hand and towards you with your bottom hand.

**7** The rod and line will fly forwards. As your top arm straightens, lift your finger off the line to release it.

**8** When the bait hits the water, reel your line back in a little so that it is tight.

## TOP TIP

Before you cast, always make sure you take a quick look around to make sure no one is standing close behind you. Then focus your eyes on where you are aiming to send your bait and then cast.

# Float fishing

Floats stop your hook sinking to the bottom, and also let you know when a fish has taken your bait. Split shots (see page 9) are used to hold the float down in the water until only the tip shows. When the float dips, it means a fish has taken a bite. There are different types of float to choose from.

## Wagglers

These floats can be used in still or running water. You thread your line through an eye or swivel only at the bottom of the waggler.

- Straight wagglers have a thicker tip and are best in moving water
- Insert wagglers have a thinner, more sensitive tip and are ideal for still waters
- Bodied wagglers are heavier and are useful if you want to cast your line further away from the bank

*Wagglers are attached by threading the line through the eye at the bottom. They are locked in place using split shot.*

## Stick floats

These floats are useful for fishing in flowing water. You attach the line to both ends and can control the float as it moves downstream. The split shot should be spread out equally between the base of the float and the hooklength.

*Stick floats are attached to the line using three float rubbers. One is attached just below the tip of the float, one halfway down and one at the bottom (see below).*

- Wire-stemmed stick floats are good in turbulent water
- Cane-stemmed floats are for fishing close to you
- Lignum-stemmed stick floats are ideal if you need to cast far out in to the water

## Surface floats

These floats (below) do not require any extra weight at all, and are used for fishing for carp on the top of the water.

*Surface floats are used by threading your line through a ring at the top of the float to keep it on the surface.*

## Predator floats

These large floats are used to suspend live or dead fish in the water. They can be attached to the line only at the bottom end. Some predator floats have a hollow tube running through the middle. When line is threaded through the tube, the float can slide along the line.

*A rubber bead and a knot tied on to the line are used to hold a sliding predator float at the exact depth you want to fish (see below).*

# Fishing on the bottom

Species that feed from the bottom of the water are hard to catch using a float. Legers or swimfeeders are used instead. Legers are weights you attach to your line to get your bait to the bottom and hold it there. Swimfeeders hold bait and attach to the end of your line. They sink to the bottom of the water.

*Bottom feeding species such as bream are best caught using legers or swimfeeders.*

## Legering

Some legers have an eye in the top through which the line goes. Other legers have holes straight through the middle, where the line is threaded.

### Bomb

*Streamlined leger for casting a long way when fishing on still waters*

### Coffin

*Flat-sided weight that holds the bait still on the bottom in flowing water*

### Bullet

*Round-shaped leger good for keeping the bait moving along the bottom in flowing water*

## KIT BITS

When your float suddenly bobs up and down in the water, you know a fish has bitten your bait. If you are fishing using a leger or swimfeeder, though, you will not have a float, but you can use a quivertip rod. This has a very fine tip, and when a fish has taken a bite, the tip pulls around, letting you know what is going on under the water.

## Block-end feeders

You can attract fish to the water where you want to fish using equipment called swimfeeders. There are two main types. Block-end feeders are plastic containers that have small holes in the sides and are blocked at both ends. You fill the swimfeeder with maggots and cast it in to the water. The feeder sinks to the bottom and the maggots escape through the holes, attracting fish to come and eat.

## Open-end feeders

This type of swimfeeder is open at both ends. You fill the feeder with groundbait, which stays in the feeder while you the cast it. When the feeder is on the bottom, the water washes it out. This leaves fish food in the water and attracts more fish to the area where your hooked bait is.

### How to fill a block-end feeder

**1** Lift the lid open and push to the side

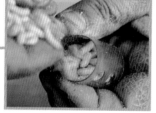

**2** Fill the feeder with maggots

**3** Snap the lid closed and cast straight away

### How to fill a groundbait feeder

**1** Push one end of your feeder into your groundbait

**2** Add some feed into the middle

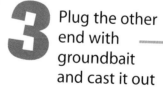

**3** Plug the other end with groundbait and cast it out

## TOP TIP

If you are fishing in clear water, fish can spook at the sight of a feeder on the bottom. A good tip is to draw a few strokes to look like weeds on the feeder, using a waterproof marker pen.

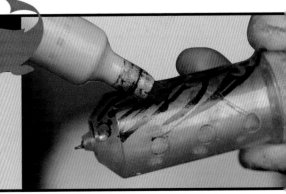

# Fishing for predators

Predators (the name for fish that eat other fish) come in many shapes and sizes. Dawn and dusk are often the best times to fish for predatory species, but you need to fish with a live or dead fish as bait, or something that mimics a swimming fish.

*A boy holds up a pike, a fierce predator common to rivers across Europe and the United States.*

## Wire traces

Predators have sharp teeth that they use to grab, hold on to and devour their prey. They can bite through a normal line so anglers use a fine wire called a trace (shown above) to catch predators. You can buy ready-made traces for fishing with live and dead fish, called 'snap tackles'. These have two hooks which are placed into the bait as shown in the pictures on the page opposite.

**DID YOU KNOW?**

Pike can grow to over 18kg, but all the big ones are females. Male pike don't grow bigger than about 4.5kg.

# Fishing with deadbaits

Some predators such as pike and catfish are scavengers, which means they eat dead fish off the bottom. You can use dead fish as bait to catch these predators. Fish you have caught from the same area you are fishing, or a sea fish such as mackerel, smelt and herrings, make very good deadbait. Catfish like pieces of bloody meat like liver, while eels will go for small fish like minnows.

# Fishing with livebaits

Using a live fish as bait is a great way to catch predators. You will need to use a float that will not be pulled under the water by your livebait but will go under when a predator fish takes a bite of the bait. When you cast it in to the water move the tip of your rod every 10 seconds or so, to help the fish spot the bait.

## How to hook a deadbait

**1** Insert the top hook of your snap tackle in the tail.

**2** Place the bottom hook in the side of the fish near the head.

**3** This is what the hooked deadbait should look like.

## How to hook a livebait

**1** Insert the top hook into the top lip.

**2** Insert the bottom hook into the flank of the fish.

**3** This is what the hooked livebait should look like.

## KIT BITS

Use a pair of long-nosed forceps or pliers to remove the hook from the mouth of a predator fish. This way you will not cut your fingers on the sharp teeth of the fish.

# Pole fishing

When you fish with a pole you simply lower the bait into the water. Poles are made of lengths of carbon that fit together, with a top section that is hollow. Pole elastic is threaded through the top. When you hook a fish the elastic line stretches out of the tip of the pole.

## Benefits of pole fishing

Fishing with a pole allows you to place the bait right where you are fishing. If you miss a bite, all you need to do is lift the pole out to check the bait is okay and lower it straight back down into the water.

### TOP TIP

Add a few drops of lubricant into the pole tip before you start fishing with your pole. This will ensure that the elastic runs smoothly through the pole while you fish.

A carbon pole ready to put together
(above) and (below) fishing using a pole.

## Buying a pole

Most poles are made from carbon fibre or glass fibre. To catch fish of lots of different sizes you can use an all-rounder pole. To catch large fish, look for a 'carp' or 'power' pole. You can also ask your tackle dealer to fit the right kind of elastic into your pole for you.

## Pole floats

There are hundreds of different pole floats to suit every type of method you might use and place you might fish. They can be broken down into two main shapes. One is called BODY UP (the main part of the body is at the top) and is ideal for rivers. The other type is called BODY DOWN (the main part of the body is at the bottom) and is ideal for still waters.

*A girl holds up a selection of different 'Body Down' pole floats.*

## KIT BITS

**Stonfo:** Plastic connector that attaches your line to the elastic

**Bush:** Soft plastic fitting that goes on the end of the pole so that the elastic can move over it smoothly

**Bung:** Sits inside the section of the pole and holds the elastic

**Elastic:** Fits to the bung inside the top sections of pole and cushions the fight of the fish

**Shipping:** Phrase used to describe moving the pole through the hands

# Getting your fish onto the bank

When you get a bite you need to set the hook in the fish's mouth. This is called striking, and it is done by moving the rod swiftly but smoothly upwards or to the side. Once a fish is hooked, start reeling it in, keeping the line to the fish tight. If the line goes slack the fish will be able to escape.

*A girl holds up a roach successfully brought to the bank.*

## Landing your catch

This boy is fishing with a swimfeeder, but these steps can be used for any type of rig.

**1** Watch for a tug on your line. This tells you a fish has taken your bait.

**2** Strike the hook by sweeping the rod back smoothly. If you are using a float, strike by sweeping the rod back over your head.

**3** Use the bend in the rod to draw the fish away from where you hooked it, making sure you keep a tight line to the fish all the time.

**4** Ease the rod back and turn the reel handle to wind in the slack. Let the fish tire itself out until it takes a gulp of air.

**5** Finally, lift the rod tip and draw the fish over the waiting net, which you should already have in the water.

## KIT BITS

Wear Polaroid sunglasses on a sunny day when you are fishing in clear waters. The sunglasses will enable you to see through the surface glare so you can spot fish in the water.

## Unhooking a fish

The first thing you should do when you catch a fish is take the hook out of its mouth. Hold the fish in one hand and the top of the hook in the other. Turn the hook round and then slide it out.

## Handling fish

Once you have caught a fish, it is very important that you handle fish in the correct way. Always wet your hands before touching any fish because they are covered with a protective slime that will rub off if they touch anything dry. If the fish is too big to hold, lay it on wet grass or a wet cloth.

## TOP TIP

If you are putting your fish back, place it in the water near where you caught it. Hold the fish under the water for a few seconds, then gently release it and let the fish swim away.

# Match Fishing

As you progress in your fishing you might want to take part in a fishing competition. This is called match fishing, and you fish against other anglers over a set period of time. The person who catches the highest weight of fish at the end is the winner.

## Stay in your place

Before the match you draw lots to decide who will fish where. You must stay in that place for the entire match. Any fish you catch of any size are added up to get your total weight at the end of the competition. Depending on local rules, certain fish may not be allowed.

## Keeping your catch

You will need to use a piece of equipment called a keepnet during the competition so all the fish you catch can be weighed up at the end. After the fish have been weighed they are put back in the water.

**DID YOU KNOW?**

The biggest fish ever caught in freshwater was a Mekong giant catfish caught in Thailand. It weighed at 293 kg – the size of a grizzly bear.

## Your first match

A good way to find out about match fishing is through a local fishing club. Here you can learn about match fishing and get started yourself because you are fishing locally with friends. Many clubs and fisheries also run matches for junior anglers during the school holidays.

# Progressing

If you are really keen on match fishing, you might like to try open matches, the next level up from match fishing. As well as the entry fee that covers the day ticket money, you will be asked to pay an additional fee. This money is shared out between the anglers with the highest weights of fish at the end of the match.

# Team fishing

Most countries hold various team competitions where you can win medals and trophies. The winners of such competitions then are invited to fish the World Club Championships, where teams from some 35 countries compete.

# International angling

The *Fédération Internationale de la Pêche Sportive* organises the World Championships. Teams of five anglers from countries all over the world compete for gold, silver and bronze, fishing to win medals either alone or in teams. The best teams in the world have come from from England, Italy, France, Hungary and Belgium.

## DID YOU KNOW?

In much of Europe matches are fished to FIPS (Fédération Internationale de la Pêche Sportiv) rules. FIPS matches are of three hours duration with any form of legering or feeder fishing banned. In the UK most matches are five hours long and legering and feeder fishing are allowed.

# Glossary/Weblinks

### Bait
Things fish like to eat. You place bait put on your hook and lower it into the water to attract fish.

### Bale arm
An arm that clicks over on the spool of your reel that collects the line onto the spool when you turn the handle.

### Bite
When a fish takes your bait.

### Boilies
Balls of paste containing eggs that have been boiled to create a tough-skinned bait taken by big fish.

### Blank
The length of carbon used to create the rod, onto which rod rings and the handle and reel seat are attached.

### Breaking strain
The amount of weight it takes to break a line.

### Butt
End of the rod holding the reel, usually covered with cork or foam and holding the reel.

### Groundbait
Bait mixed with water, rolled into balls and placed into a swimfeeder.

### Float fishing
Fishing using a float as bite indication.

### Keepnet
Net used to keep your catch until the end of the session. These are banned in Germany.

### Legering
Catching fish that feed on the bottom of the water.

### Livebaiting
The use of live fish as bait to target predatory fish.

### Spool
This is where the line sits on your reel. Most reels come with more than one spool and they are easily interchanged.

### Shot
Weights with splits though the centre, which are squeezed onto the line to weigh down floats or in larger sizes are used as light leger weights.

### Striking
Lifting the top of your rod to make sure the hook goes into the fish's mouth when you get a bite.

### Swimfeeder
Device used to hold groundbait when fishing on the bottom to get feed close to your hook bait.

### Waggler
Type of float which can be used on still and running water.

# Rules and regulations

Each country and region will have its own rules regarding licences and the list below offers a guide of what to expect. Many countries have periods in which you are not allowed to fish for certain species, usually to allow the fish time to lay eggs and increase their populations.

## England and Wales

Everyone over the age of 12 needs a National Rod Licence issued by the Environmental Agency and sold through post offices. Fishing for coarse fish is not allowed on rivers between 14 March and 16 June. However, fishing is allowed on most still waters and many canals.

## United States

There is no national licence but each state requires a state government licence to fish in freshwater. There are closed seasons for bass, walleye, pike and muskies, especially in the northern states.

## France

You can fish anywhere all year round. Each region issues its own permit and no national licence required.

## Republic of Ireland

There is no closed season. You do not need a licence to fish in Ireland, although fishing with live bait is banned.

## Germany

There is no closed season for general coarse fishing but you cannot fish for pike from January to April or for zander from April to June. Germans have to sit an exam before they can get a fishing licence and in some parts of the country no fish can be returned alive. Keepnets are banned.

## Scandanavia

Usually you just need a local licence to fish. You can buy this at tourist offices and tackle shops, and you can fish year round, although in winter most places will be frozen over.

## Spain

There is no closed season here but bans can be imposed on fishing when water levels drop very low in hot weather. Local tackle shops supply the required licences. Night fishing is banned on many rivers.

## Italy

Each species has a period during which you can't fish for them around April to June, when they are spawning. These vary depending on where you are. You'll need a photograph and proof of ID to get a licence, but it will last you for six years. Night fishing is usually banned.

# Weblinks

**www.environment-agency.gov.uk**
This site explains the work of the Environmental Agency. You can also buy your England and Wales licences online here.

**www.watfaa.iinet.net.au**
Website for the Australian Trout And Freshwater Angling Association.

**www.total-fishing.com**
Excellent site for pleasure and match anglers.

**www.thecarpsociety.com**
Official site of the UK Carp Society.

**www.cips-fips.org**
Website for the governing body of competitive angling in Europe.

**www.nfadirect.com**
Website for the National Federation of Anglers (England).

**www.total-fishingclub.com**
Excellent subscription site with hundreds of top quality angling articles.

**www.pacgb.co.uk**
The Pike Anglers Club of Great Britain website.

**www.bassfishingusa.com**
US site for lovers of large- and small-mouth bass.

**www.asafishing.org**
American Sportfishing Association website.

**www.mickthill.com**
Site for the American Fishing Association.

# Index